Scrunch Your Butt Cheeks!

How little Bobby got his smile back.

Written by
Bob Stead, M.S., LPC

Illustrated by
Toby Mikle

Dedication

This book is dedicated to all of my clients over the years. You have shown me what determination and perseverance look like as you fight your personal battles. I am inspired daily to be the best version of myself, so that I can be an example for all those to follow.

Little Bobby was always angry, and he couldn't figure out why.

When his parents would wake him up in the morning
he would yell and stomp, "why do I have to wake up".

When it was time for breakfast sometimes little Bobby would be angry,
Why do I have
to eat that?

When it was time to go to school little Bobby would scream,

At school little Bobby would get frustrated
when his teacher gave assignments,

At recess little Bobby was always angry that other kids wouldn't play his games, "but I don't want to play your game", little Bobby would yell.

When little Bobby came home from school,
he would be angry for so many things,

I didn't get the right snack!

I want to watch something different!

I want to play
with my friends!

No matter what little Bobby was doing he was always so frustrated.

One day little Bobby's parents brought him to a new building,
inside was a new office, and there he met his new friend.

Little's Bobby's friend was a counselor and wanted to learn
all about what made little Bobby so angry.

Little Bobby talked about all the things that made him angry and then.........

Little Bobby's new counselor asked him to try something completely new.

Every time you start to get frustrated scrunch your butt cheeks and count to 5.

When you get to 5 relax and take a DEEP breath.

Little Bobby though this sounded so silly
and shook his head back and forth.

I'm not doing that" little Bobby grumbled.

The counselor smiled and said, "OK, but I'm feeling better already"!

Little Bobby crossed his arms and said,
"fine, but only once".

Little Bobby did what the counselor said, and the first time he didn't feel that much better, but he felt something...........

Then, after little Bobby practiced with his new friend the counselor a few more times something really strange started to happen.

When little Bobby would tighten and release those
muscles, sure enough, he would start to smile.

First just a smirk, then a grin, then a giggle, and before you could yell SQUEEZE, little Bobby had the biggest grin.

Little Bobby didn't really know why he was feeling angry, and now little Bobby doesn't know why he is feeling happy, He. Just. Is!

So now, whenever little Bobby starts to get angry, frustrated, anxious, or scared, he knows just what to do.

Scrunch your butt cheeks he yells, and the giggles come rolling down.

And the best part is that little Bobby's parents can do it too!